Intellect and th

Prof. Michael Bank

bankmichael1@gmail.com

To order additional copies of this book, contact
Toll Free +65 3165 7531 (Singapore)
Toll Free +60 3 3099 4412 (Malaysia)
www.partridgepublishing.com/singapore
orders.singapore@partridgepublishing.com

ISBN
ISBN: 978-1-5437-7369-9 (sc)
ISBN: 978-1-5437-7371-2 (hc)
ISBN: 978-1-5437-7370-5 (e)

Print information available on the last page.

03/30/2023

PARTRIDGE

The present album is an attempt to trace a connection between intellect and city architecture.

The architecture of Saint Petersburg (Petersburg further on) was taken as an example. The city is about 300 years old. According to Alexander Pushkin, Tsar Peter the Great had founded this place as a "Window to Europe", but the city had obviously grown into a wide gate rather than a window. Huge scientific and cultural contribution has been made to the whole world through this gate.

The population of this city was about one million people in the 19th century. It was situated in a country which could hardly be called rich, considering the amount of "poor people" (see title of Feodor Dostoevsky's novel). And yet, Petersburg has always been one of the most cultural cities in the world.

Wonderful architecture of Petersburg is well known to have influenced life and character of people living there. This fact was depicted in classic literature repeatedly. And in turn city inhabitants influenced its development creating new scientific institutions, libraries, museums, theatres and concert halls.

Only the well-known scientists and cultural workers, whose life and activity were at least partially connected with Petersburg, are mentioned here. The places of interest reminding us of these extraordinary people and their heritage are shown alongside.

Of course it's impossible to include all the remarkably talented scientists, musicians, painters and writers who are not widely known in the world due to the language barrier, former political regime, the iron curtain and not always objective attitude to the Russian culture.

But even the concise list of the names mentioned here strikes by the intense intellectual power concentrated in a relatively small but incredibly beautiful city.

All photos besides those marked by @ are made by author. All biographical data is taken from Wikipedia.

Contents

1. Peter the Great legacy 2

2. Writers 12

3. Scientists 26

4. Composers 44

5. Musicians 56

6. Ballet 62

7. Jeweler's art 72

8. Russian avant-garde 82

9. Sport and Art 90

10. Epilogue 100

1. Peter the Great legacy

Peter the Great or Pyotr I, (9 June 1672 – 8 February 1725)[1] ruled Russia and later the Russian Empire from 7 May 1682 until his death, jointly ruling before 1696 with his weak and sickly half-brother, Ivan V. Peter the Great carried out a policy of Westernization and expansion that transformed the Tsardom of Russia into the 3-billion acre Russian Empire, a major European power.

"New Holland"

In Peter and Paul Fortress.

2. Writers

Alexander Sergeevich Pushkin (June 6 1799–February 10 1837) was a Russian author of the Romantic era who is considered to be the greatest Russian poet and the founder of modern Russian literature. Pushkin pioneered the use of vernacular speech in his poems and plays, creating a style of storytelling—mixing drama, romance, and satire—associated with Russian literature ever since and greatly influencing later Russian writers.

Nikolai Vasilievich Gogol (1 April 1809, – 4 March 1852) was a Ukrainian-born Russian writer. His works belong to the tradition of Russian literature; often called the "father of modern Russian realism" he was one of the first Russian authors to criticize his country's way of life. The play The Inspector-General (1836, 1842), and the short stories Diary of a Madman, The Nose and The Overcoat (1842) are among his best known works. With their scrupulous and scathing realism, ethical criticism as well as philosophical depth, they remain some of the most important works of world literature.

Fyodor Mikhaylovich Dostoyevsky (November 11 1821 – February 9 1881) was a Russian fiction writer, essayist and philosopher whose works include Crime and Punishment and The Brothers Karamazov. Dostoyevsky is recognized as one of the greatest and most influential writers of all time.

Iosif Aleksandrovich Brodsky (24 May 1940 – 28 January 1996) was a Russian poet and essayist and Nobel Laureate in Literature.

He was appointed Poet Laureate Consultant in Poetry to the Library of Congress in 1991. At an interview in Stockholm airport, to the question: “You are an American citizen who is receiving the Prize for Russian-language poetry. Who are you, an American or a Russian?”, he responded: “I am Jewish - a Russian poet and an English essayist”.

Ivan Sergeyevich Turgenev (November 9 1818 – September 3 1883) was a Russian novelist and playwright. His novel Fathers and Sons is regarded as one of the major works of 19th-century fiction.

Vladimir Vladimirovich Nabokov (23 April 1899, Saint Petersburg – 2 July 1977, Montreux) was a multilingual Russian-American novelist and short story writer. Nabokov wrote his first nine novels in Russian, then rose to international prominence as a master English prose stylist. He also made contributions to entomology and had an interest in chess problems. Nabokov's Lolita (1955) is frequently cited as amongst his most important novels, and is his most widely known, exhibiting the love of intricate wordplay and descriptive detail that characterized all his works. The novel was ranked at #4 in the list of the 100 best novels of the 20th century by the Modern Library

The Pushkin`s Lyceum

The Pushkin`s Lyceum

"Engineer Castle" – Dostoevsky School

The Raskolnikov`s house

Way to murder

The money-lender old woman house

3. Scientists

Leonhard Paul Euler (15 April 1707 – 18 September 1783) was a pioneering Swiss mathematician and physicist who spent most of his life in Russia and Germany. Around this time Johann Bernoulli's two sons, Daniel and Nicolas, were working at the Imperial Russian Academy of Sciences in St Petersburg. Euler worked in almost all areas of mathematics: geometry, calculus, trigonometry, algebra, and number theory, as well as continuum physics, lunar theory and other areas of physics.

Heinrich Friedrich Emil Lenz (February 12, 1804 - February 10, 1865) was a Baltic German physicist most famous for formulating Lenz's law in 1833. Lenz began working at the University of St. Petersburg, where he later served as Dean of Mathematics and Physics from 1840 to 1863 and Rector from 1863 until his death in 1865. He began studying electromagnetism in 1831.

Besides the law named in his honor, Lenz also independently discovered Joule's law in 1842; to honor his efforts on the problem, it is also given the name the "Joule-Lenz law".

Daniel Bernoulli (Groningen, 29 January 1700 – 27 July 1782) was a Dutch-Swiss mathematician and was one of the many prominent mathematicians in the Bernoulli family. He is particularly remembered for his applications of mathematics to mechanics, especially fluid mechanics, and for his pioneering work in probability and statistics. Bernoulli's work is still studied at length by many schools of science throughout the world.

Portrait of Mendeleev by Ilya Repin

Dmitri Ivanovich Mendeleev (8 February 1834 – 2 February 1907), was a Russian chemist and inventor. He is credited as being the creator of the first version of the periodic table of elements. Using the table, he predicted the properties of elements yet to be discovered.

о053вт 70

Ivan **Pavlov (the Nobel Prize laureate1904)** He is widely known for first describing the phenomenon of classical conditioning

Pafnuty Lvovich **Chebyshev** (May 16 1821 – December 8 1894)[1] was a Russian mathematician. Chebyshev is known for his work in the field of probability, statistics and number theory. According to the Mathematics Genealogy Project, Chebyshev has about 5,000 mathematical “descendants”. The crater Chebyshev on the Moon and the asteroid 2010 Chebyshev are named in his honour.

Vladimir Andreevich Steklov (January 9, 1864 – May 30, 1926) was a Soviet/Russian mathematician, mechanician and physicist. Steklov's primary scientific contribution is in the area of orthogonal functional sets. He introduced a class of closed orthogonal sets; developed asymptotic Liouville-Steklov's method for orthogonal polynomials; proved theorems on generalized Fourier series. Steklov developed approximation technique later named Steklov function. He also worked on hydrodynamics and theory of elasticity.

Alexander Stepanovich Popov (March 16 1859 – January 13 1905] 1906) was a Russian physicist who first demonstrated the practical application of electromagnetic (radio) waves, although he did not apply for a patent for his invention. Beginning in the early 1890s he continued the experiments of other radio pioneers, such as Heinrich Hertz. In 1894 he built his first radio receiver, a version of the coherer. Further refined as a lightning detector, it was presented to the Russian Physical and Chemical Society on May 7, 1895 — the day has been celebrated in the Russian Federation as "Radio Day". The paper on his findings was published the same year. In March 1896, he effected transmission of radio waves between different campus buildings in St Petersburg.

Aleksandr Mikhailovich Lyapunov June 6 1857 – November 3, 1918) was a Russian mathematician, mechanician and physicist. His work in the field of differential equations, potential theory, the stability of systems and probability theory is very important. His main preoccupations were the stability of equilibria and the motion of mechanical systems, the model theory for the stability of uniform turbulent liquid, and particles under the influence of gravity. His work in the field of mathematical physics was very important for subsequent advances of this field.

Nikolay Semenov (the Nobel Prize laureate in Chemistry 1956) Semenov has made valuable contributions to the field of molecular physics; he has also carried out investigations on electron phenomena, dielectric breakdown and the propagation of explosive waves.

Aleksandr Mikhailovich Prokhorov (the Nobel Prize laureate 1964). He made contribution in developing the electronic paramagnetic resonance.

Kapitza Pyotr Leonidovich (the Nobel Prize laureate 1978) It is known his studie of high-power electronics and plasma physics

Ilya Ilyich Mechnikov (the Nobel Prize laureate1908). He was a Russian microbiologist best remembered for his pioneering research into the immune system.

The University

Lev Davidovich Landau was a prominent Soviet physicist who made fundamental contributions to many areas of theoretical physics. He received the 1962 Nobel Prize in Physics for his development of a mathematical theory of superfluidity

Zhores Alferov (the Nobel Prize laureate 2000). who contributed significantly to the creation of modern heterostructure physics and electronics.

Pavel **Cherenkov**In 1958 he was awarded the **Nobel Prize** in Physics for the discovery of the Cherenkov effect.

Grigori Yakovlevich **Perelman** born 13 June 1966 in Leningrad, USSR (now St. Petersburg, Russia), sometimes known as Grisha Perelman, is a Russian mathematician who has made landmark contributions to Riemannian geometry and geometric topology. In particular, he proved Thurston's geometrization conjecture. In August 2006, Perelman was awarded the Fields Medal for "his contributions to geometry and his revolutionary insights into the analytical and geometric structure of the Ricci flow". Perelman declined to accept the award or to appear at the congress. On 22 December 2006, the journal Science recognized Perelman's proof of the Poincaré Conjecture as the scientific "Breakthrough of the Year," the first such recognition in the area of mathematics.

Vladimir Ilyich Lenin 22 April 1870 - 21 January 1924), and also known by the pseudonyms V.I. Lenin and N. Lenin, was a Russian revolutionary, a communist politician, His contributions to Marxist theory are commonly referred to as Leninism. Leninism refers to various related political and economic theories elaborated by Bolshevik revolutionary leader Vladimir Lenin. Leninism builds upon and elaborates the ideas of Marxism, and serves as a philosophical basis for the ideology of Soviet Communism.

Wassily Leontief (the Nobel Prize laureate 1973) He develops the most important directions of the modern economic theory - Analysis of the interbranch communications.

Leonid Kantorovich (the Nobel Prize laureate 1975). He is known for his theory and development of techniques for the optimal allocation of resources.

The Public Library

Igor **Sikorsky** (25 May 1889 – 26 October 1972). Sikorsky was a Russian-American pioneer of aviation who designed and flew the world's first multi-engine fixed-wing aircraft, developed the first of Pan American Airways' ocean-conquering flying boats in the 1930s. Sikorsky was highly influential in the development of helicopters, founding the Sikorsky Aircraft Corporation, one of today's leading helicopter manufacturers. In 1942, the Sikorsky R-4 became the world's first production helicopter, pioneering a rotor layout used by most helicopters today. Sikorsky began studying at the Saint Petersburg Imperial Russian Naval Academy, in 1903, at the age of 14. In Spring 1912, Igor Sikorsky became Chief Engineer of the aircraft division for the Russian Baltic Railroad Car Works in Saint Petersburg. In 1914, he was awarded an honorary degree in engineering from Saint Petersburg Polytechnical Institute. In 1928, Sikorsky became a naturalized citizen of the United States. The Sikorsky Aircraft Corporation in Stratford, Connecticut, continues to the present day as one of the world's leading helicopter manufacturers, and a nearby small airport has been named Sikorsky Airport.

Vladimir Kozmich Zworykin (July 30, 1889 - July 29, 1982) was a Russian-Americaninventor, engineer, and pioneer of television technology. Zworykin invented a television transmitting and receiving system employing cathode ray tubes, He studied at the St. Petersburg Institute of Technology, under Boris Rosing, According to recently discovered accumulated personal correspondence of Zworykin, he helped Boris Rosing with experimental work on television in the basement of Rosing's private lab at the School of Anillery of Saint Petersburg, Russia.

Vladimir Zworykin, 1929, holding his kinescope

4. Composers

Mikhail Ivanovich Glinka (June 1 1804 – February 15 1857), was the first Russian composer to gain wide recognition inside his own country, and is often regarded as the father of Russian classical music.

Glinka's compositions were an important influence on future Russian composers, notably the members of The Five, who took Glinka's lead and produced a distinctively Russian kind of romantic (classical) music.

Pyotr Ilyich Tchaikovsky (May 1840 – November 1893) was a Russian composer of the Romantic era. Tchaikovsky became a dominant figure in 19th century Russian music and known both in and outside Russia as a great musical talent. His formal conservatory training instilled in him Western-oriented attitudes and techniques, allowing him to show a wide range and breadth of technique. This breadth ranged from a poised "Classical" form simulating 18th century Rococo elegance to a style more characteristic of Russian nationalists or forming a musical idiom as a channel to express his own overwrought emotions.

Modest Petrovich **Mussorgsky** (March 21 1839 – March 28 1881), one of the Russian composers known as the Five, was an innovator of Russian music. He strove to achieve a uniquely Russian musical identity, often in deliberate defiance of the established conventions of Western music. Many of his major works were inspired by Russian history, Russian folklore, and other nationalist themes, including the opera Boris Godunov, the orchestral tone poem Night on Bald Mountain, and the piano suite Pictures at an Exhibition.

Sergei Vasilievich **Rachmaninoff** (1 April 1873– 28 March 1943) was a Russian composer, pianist, and conductor. He was one of the finest pianists of his day and, as a composer, the last great representative of Russian late Romanticism in classical music

Alexander Porfiryevich Borodin (12 November 1833 – 27 February 1887) was a Russian composer of Georgian-Russian parentage who made his living as a notable chemist. He was a member of the group of composers called The Five (or "The Mighty Handful"), who were dedicated to producing a specifically Russian kind of art music. He is best known for his symphonies, his two string quartets, and his opera Prince Igor.

Ottorino Respighi (July 9, 1879 - April 18, 1936) was an Italian composer, musicologist and conductor. He is best known for his orchestral Roman trilogy: "Fountains of Rome"; "Pines of Rome"; and "Roman Festivals". His musicological interest in 16th-, 17th- and 18th-century music led him to also compose pieces based on the music of this period. Born in Bologna, he studied composition with Giuseppe Martucci, and briefly with Max Bruch and Nikolai Rimsky-Korsakov.

Principally a violinist until 1908, he then turned primarily to composition.

Nikolai Andreyevich Rimsky-Korsakov (18 March 1844 – 21 June 1908) was a Russian composer, and a member of the group of composers known as "The Five." He is particularly noted for a predilection for folk and fairy-tale subjects, and for his extraordinary skill in orchestration, which may have been influenced by his synesthesia. Although he expended his greatest efforts on his 15 operas, Rimsky- Korsakov's reputation in the West has long been based on his best-known orchestral compositions— Capriccio espagnol, Russian Easter Festival Overture, and the symphonic suite Scheherazade

Igor Fyodorovich Stravinsky (17 June 1882 – 6 April 1971) was a Russian-born composer, considered by many to be the most influential composer of 20th century music. He was a quintessentially cosmopolitan Russian who was named by Time magazine as one of the 100 most influential people of the century. Stravinsky's compositional career was notable for its stylistic diversity. He first achieved international fame with three ballets commissioned by the impresario Sergei Diaghilev and performed by Diaghilev's Ballets Russes (Russian Ballets): "The Firebird" (1910), Petrushka (1911/1947), and "The Rite of Spring" (1913).

THE MARIINSKY THEATRE

Alexander Nikolayevich Scriabin (6 January 1872 -27 April 1915) was a Russian composer and pianist who developed a highly lyrical and idiosyncratic tonal language. Driven by a poetic, philosophical and aesthetic vision that bordered on the mystical, he can be considered the primary figure of Russian Symbolism in music.

Portrait of Glazunov by Repin

Aleksandr Konstantinovich Glazunov 10 August 1865 – 21 March 1936) was a composer, music teacher and conductor. He served as director of the Saint Petersburg Conservatory between 1905 and 1928. He continued heading the Conservatory until 1930, though he had left the Soviet Union in 1928 and did not return. The best known student under his tenure during the early Soviet years was Dmitri Shostakovich.

Anton Grigorevich **Rubinstein** (November 28, 1829 – November 20, 1894) was a Russian pianist, composer and conductor. As a pianist he was regarded as a rival of Franz Liszt, and he ranks amongst the great keyboard virtuosos. He also founded the Saint Petersburg Conservatory, which, together with Moscow Conservatory founded by his brother Nikolai Rubinstein, helped establish a reputation for musical skill among the subjects of the Tsar of Russia.

Sergei Sergeyevich **Prokofiev** (27 April 1891 - 5 March 1953) was a Russian composer who mastered numerous musical genres and came to be admired as one of the greatest composers of the 20th century. Today, this is one of Prokofiev's best-known works, and it contains some of the most inspired and poignant passages in his whole output.

Dmitri Dmitriyevich **Shostakovich** (25 September 1906 – 9 August 1975) was a Russian composer of the Soviet period. After a period influenced by Prokofiev and Stravinsky (e.g. in his Symphony No. 1 of 1927), Shostakovich developed a hybrid of styles as exemplified in his opera Lady Macbeth of the Mtsensk District (1934) and a form of post-romantic style (after Mahler). This aspect of Shostakovich's technique owes more to Gustav Mahler than Rimsky-Korsakov. His most popular works are his 15 symphonies and 15 string quartets. His works for piano include 2 piano sonatas, an early set of preludes, and a later set of 24 preludes and fugues. Other works include two operas, six concertos, and a substantial quantity of film music.

THE MARIINSKY THEATRE

THE MARIINSKY THEATRE

It is possible to take from site'7'he 100 Grates Composers": http:lldiqitaldrean1door.nutsle.con1/paqeslbest-classic-con1p.htn1l list of Grate Composers born after 1870.

10. Igor Stravinsky-1882-1971 Petersburg
22. Serge Prokofiev -1891-1953 Petersburg
23. Dmitri Shostakovich -1906-1975 Petersburg
29. Maurice Ravel -1875-1937 Madrid Paris
36. Sergei Rachmaninoff -1873-1943 Petersburg
46. Arnold Schoenberg -1874-1951 Vienna
47. Charles Ives -1874-1954 Danbury, Connecticut
48. Paul Hindemith - 1895-1963 Frankfurt amMain
49. Olivier Messiaen - 1908-1992 Paris
50. Aaron Copland - 1900-1990 Brooklyn
54. Benjamin Britten -1913-1976 Lowestoft, Suffolk
57. Alexander Scriabin -1872-1915 Petersburg
61. Anton Webern -1883-1945 Vienna
63. George Gershwin -1898-1937 Brooklyn
72. Alban Berg - 1885-1935 Vienna
76. Francis Poulenc -1899-1963 Paris
80. John Cage -1912-1992Los Angeles_.
83. Gustav Holst-1874-1934 London ,.
85. Ottorino Respighi -1879-1936 Bologna
89. William Walton -1902-1983 Oldham, Lancashire.
90.Darius Milhaud - 1892-1974 Paris ,
93.Samuel Barber -1910-1981 West Chester
96.Manuel de Falla -1876-1946 Madrid

AT ULili1£

Conclusion: Every fourth or fifth Great Composer in the 19-th century is from Petersburg!

In center Alexandrinsky Theatre is the oldest professional theatre in Russia

5. Musicians

Leopold Auer (June 7, 1845 – July 15, 1930) was a Hungarian violinist, teacher, conductor and composer. On a visit to London in 1868, he was invited to perform Beethoven's Archduke Trio with pianist Anton Rubinstein and cellist Alfredo Piatti. Rubinstein was in search for a violin professor for the Saint Petersburg Conservatory and he suggested Auer. Auer agreed to a three year contract; he would actually stay for 49 years. Auer is remembered as one of the most important pedagogues of the violin, and was one of the most sought-after teachers for gifted pupils.

Many famous virtuoso violinists were among his pupils, including Mischa Elman, Jascha Heifetz, Nathan Milstein, Efrem Zimbalist, Georges Boulanger, Benno Rabinof, Kathleen Parlow, Oscar Shumsky, and Shinichi Suzuki.

The great Russian bass singer, Feodor Ivanovich Shaliapin (1873 - 1938), is still famous throughout the world. He has been rightfully considered one of the greatest performers ever. Considered the greatest dramatic singer of his day, he was largely self-taught. He sang Russian opera, notably Mussorgsky and Rimsky-Korsakov, in Russia during the period 1893 - 1901. He then toure Europe, extending his repertoire. He emigrated from Russia in 1922, after the Revolution, and lived abroad, singing in Metropolitene, Paris Opera, and throughout the world. He died in Paris on 12th April 1938.

Jascha Heifetz was a Jewish violin virtuoso born in Lithuania (February 2 1901 – December 10, 1987). He is hailed as the greatest violinist of the 20th century. In 1910 he entered the Saint Petersburg Conservatory to study under Leopold Auer. He had performed with the Chicago Symphony Orchestra, London Symphony Orchestra, and the Boston Symphony Orchestra.

Zimbalist was born in the southwestern Russian city the son of Jewish parents Maria and Aron Zimbalist, who was a conductor. By the age of nine, Efrem Zimbalist was first violin in his father's orchestra. At age 12 he entered the Saint Petersburg Conservatory and studied under Leopold Auer. He graduated from the St. Petersburg Conservatory in 1907 after winning a gold medal and the Rubenstein Prize, and by age 21 was considered one of the world's greatest violinists.

Yevgeny Aleksandrovich Mravinsky (4 June 1903 – 19 January 1988) was a Russian conductor. In October 1938, Mravinsky took up the post that he was to hold until 1988: principal conductor of the Leningrad Philharmonic Orchestra, with whom he had made his debut as a conductor in 1931. Under Mravinsky, the Leningrad Philharmonic gained a legendary reputation, particularly in Russian music such as Tchaikovsky and Shostakovich. Mravinsky gave world premieres of six symphonies by Shostakovich: numbers 5, 6, 8 (which Shostakovich dedicated to Mravinsky), 9, 10 and finally 12 in 1961.

Valery Abisalovich Gergiev (born 2 May 1953) is a Russian conductor and opera company director. He is general director and artistic director of the Mariinsky Theatre, principal conductor of the London Symphony Orchestra, and principal guest conductor of the Metropolitan Opera. Valery Gergiev is the artistic director of the White Nights Festival in St. Petersburg.

Yuri Khatuevich Temirkanov (born 10 December 1938) has been the Music Director and Chief Conductor of the Saint Petersburg Philharmonic since 1988. In addition to leading the Saint Petersburg Philharmonic, Maestro Temirkanov served as the Baltimore Symphony Orchestra's 11th Music Director from 2000 until 2006 and is currently the Principal Guest Conductor of the Danish National Symphony Orchestra and Conductor Laureate of the Royal Philharmonic Orchestra in London.

Anna Yur'yevna Netrebko born September 18, 1971 (1971-09-18) (age 37) in Krasnodar. Under Gergiev's guidance, Netrebko made her operatic stage debut at the Mariinsky as Susanna in Le Nozze di Figaro. She went on to sing many prominent roles with the Kirov Opera, including Amina in La Sonnambula, Pamina in Die Zauberflöte, Rosina in Il Barbiere di Siviglia, and Lucia in Lucia di Lammermoor.

The Saint-Petersburg Philharmonic

6. Ballet

Marius Ivanovich **Petipa** (born on 11 March 1818 in Marseille, Kingdom of France — died in Gurzuf in the Crimea, was a ballet dancer, teacher, and choreographer. Marius Petipa is noted for his long career as Premier Maître de Ballet of the St. Petersburg Imperial Theatres, a position he held from 1871 until 1903. Petipa created over fifty ballets, some of which have survived in versions either faithful to, inspired by, or reconstructed from the original — The Pharaoh's Daughter (1862); Don Quixote (1869); La Bayadère (1877); Le Talisman (1889); The Sleeping Beauty (1890); The Nutcracker (which was possibly choreographed by Lev Ivanov, with Petipa's counsel and instruction) (1892); Le réveil de Flore (1894); Le Halte de Cavalerie (1896); Raymonda (1898); Les Saisons (1900), and Les millions d'Arlequin (a.k.a. Harlequinade) (1900).

Anna Pavlovna **Pavlova** (12 February 1881–23 January 1931) was a Russian ballerina of the late 19th and the early 20th century. She is widely regarded as one of the most famous classical ballet dancers in history and was most noted as a Principal artist of the Imperial Russian Ballet and the Ballets Russes of Serge Diaghilev. Pavlova is most recognised for the creation of the role The Dying Swan and with her own company, would become the first ballerina to tour ballet around the world.

Sergei Pavlovich Diaghilev (March 31, 1872 – August 19, 1929) was a Russian art critic, patron, ballet impresario and founder of the Ballets Russes from which many famous dancers and choreographers would later arise.

Portrait of Diaghilev by Serov

George Balanchine (January 22, 1904 – April 30, 1983), born Giorgi Melitonis dze Balanchivadze in Saint Petersburg, Russia, to Georgian parents, was one of the 20th century's foremost choreographers, a pioneer of ballet in the United States, co- founder and balletmaster of New York City Ballet: his work created modern ballet, based on his deep knowledge of classical forms and techniques. He was a choreographer known for his musicality; he did not illustrate music but expressed it in dance and worked extensively with Igor Stravinsky, his contemporary.

The Vaganova Ballet School

Galina Sergeyevna Ulánova (8 January 1910 - 21 March 1998) is frequently cited as being one of the greatest 20th Century ballerinas.

Ulanova studied in Petrograd under Agrippina Vaganova and her own mother, a ballerina of the Imperial Russian Ballet. When she joined the Mariinsky Theatre in 1928, the press found in her "much of Semyonova's style, grace, the same exceptional plasticity and a sort of captivating modesty in her gestures". In 1944, when her fame reached Stalin, he had her transferred to the Bolshoi Theatre, where she would be the prima ballerina assoluta for 16 years.

Rudolf Khametovich Nureyev (March 17, 1938 – January 6, 1993) was a Siberian dancer, primarily known for his work in ballet. He was accepted by the Leningrad Choreographic School (1955), the associate school of the Kirov Ballet. In his three years with the Kirov, he danced fifteen roles, usually opposite his partner, Ninel Kurgapkina, with whom he was very well paired, although she was almost a decade older than he. He became one of the Soviet Union's best-known dancers and was allowed to travel outside the Soviet Union, when he danced in Vienna at the International Youth Festival. Not long after, for disciplinary reasons, he was told he would not be allowed to go abroad again.

Rudolf Nureyev and Margot Fonteyn

Yury Nikolayevich Grigorovich (born January 2, 1927 in Leningrad) is a Russian dancer and choreographer who dominated the Russian ballet for 30 years. After the death of his wife, the great ballerina Natalia Bessmertnova, on February 19, 2008, he has been offered the opportunity to return to the Bolshoi again in the capacity of ballet master and choreographer.

Mikhail Nikolaevich Baryshnikov (born January 27, 1948) is a Soviet-born Russian American dancer, choreographer, and actor, often cited alongside Vaslav Nijinsky and Rudolf Nureyev as one of the greatest ballet dancers of the 20th century. After a promising start in the Kirov Ballet in Leningrad, he defected to Canada in 1974 for more opportunities in western dance. After freelancing with many companies, he joined the New York City Ballet as a principal dancer to learn George Balanchine's style of movement. He then moved to dance and later became artistic director with the American Ballet Theatre, also in New York.

Nataliya Romanovna Makarova (born November 21, 1940) is a Soviet-Russian-born American actress and former prima ballerina. Makarova was born in Leningrad in former Soviet Russia. At the age of 12, she auditioned for the Leningrad Choreographic School (formerly the Imperial Ballet School), and was accepted although most students join the school at the age of 10. She was a permanent member of the Kirov Ballet in Leningrad from 1956 to 1970, achieving prima ballerina status during the 1960s. Soon after Makarova defected to the West in 1970, she began performing with the American Ballet Theatre in New York and the Royal Ballet in London.

7. Jeweler's art

Bouquet of Lilies by Fabergé

Peter Carl Fabergé (May 30 1846 – September 24 1920) was a Russian jeweller, best known for the famous Fabergé eggs, made in the style of genuine Easter eggs, but using precious metals and gemstones rather than more mundane materials. He was born in Saint Petersburg. He became the Tsar's Court Goldsmith in 1885. The Imperial Easter eggs were a sideline; Fabergé made many more objects ranging from silver tableware to fine jewelry.

Fabergé's company became the largest in Russia, with 500 employees and branches in Saint Petersburg, Moscow, Odessa, Kiev and London. In 1897 the Swedish court appointed Fabergé Court Goldsmith. In 1900 his work represented Russia at the 1900 World's Fair in Paris.

The amber's room.

8. Russian avant-garde

Malevich. Black Squer

Nathan Isaevich Altman (December 22 1889 – December 12, 1970) was a Russian avant-garde artist, Cubist painter, stage designer and book illustrator. In 1925 he participated in Exposition Internationale des Arts Decoratifs et Industriels Moderns (Art Deco) in Paris together with Aleksandra Ekster, Vadim Meller, Sonia Delaunay-Terk and David Shterenberg. His first solo exhibition in Leningrad was in 1926. Altman moved to Paris in 1928. In 1936 he returned to Leningrad. He worked mainly for the theatre, as a book illustrator and an author of essays about art.

Portrait of Anna Akhmatova by Altman

Kazimir Severinovich **Malevich** (February 23, 1878 – May 15, 1935) was a painter and art theoretician, pioneer of geometric abstract art and the originator of the Avant-garde Suprematist movement. On November 3, 2008 a work by Malevich entitled Suprematist Composition from 1916 set the world record for any Russian work of art and any work sold at auction for that year, selling at Sotheby's in New York City for just over $60 million U.S. (far surpassing his previous record of $17 million set in 2000).

Aleksander Mikhailovich **Rodchenko** (5 December 1891 – December 3, 1956) was a Russian artist, sculptor, photographer and graphic designer. He was one of the founders of constructivism and Russian design. Rodchenko was one of the most versatile Constructivist and Productivist artists to emerge after the Russian Revolution. He worked as a painter and graphic designer before turning to photomontage and photography. His photography was socially engaged, formally innovative, and opposed to a painterly aesthetic. Concerned with the need for analytical-documentary photo series, he often shot his subjects from odd angles—usually high above or below—to shock the viewer and to postpone recognition. He wrote: "One has to take several different shots of a subject, from different points of view and in different situations, as if one examined it in the round rather than looked through the same key-hole again and again."

Rodchenko with his wife Stepanova

The Russian Museum

ЗОЛОТОЙ
СОФИТ

9. Sport and Art

Mikhail Moiseyevich Botvinnik (August 17 1911 – May 5, 1995) was a Russian International Grandmaster and long- time World Chess Champion. As an electrical engineer, he was one of the very few famous chess players who achieved distinction in another career while playing top-class competitive chess. Botvinnik was the first world-class player to develop within the Soviet Union Botvinnik also played a major role in the organization of chess, making a significant contribution to the design of the World Chess Championship system. His famous pupils include World Champions Anatoly Karpov, Garry Kasparov and Vladimir Kramnik.

Boris Vasilievich Spassky (born January 30, 1937) is a Russian-French chess grandmaster. He was the tenth World Chess Champion, holding the title from 1969 to 1972. Spassky won the Soviet Chess Championship twice outright (1961, 1973), and twice more lost in playoffs (1956, 1963), after tying for first during the event proper. He was a World Chess Championship Candidate on seven occasions (1956, 1965, 1968, 1974, 1977, 1980, and 1985).

Viktor Lvovich Korchnoi born March 23, 1931, in Leningrad, USSR) is a professional Swiss chess player and currently the oldest active grandmaster on the world tournament circuit. Korchnoi is also a chess author. In all, Korchnoi was a Candidate for the World Championship on ten occasions (1962, 1968, 1971, 1974, 1977, 1980, 1983, 1985, 1988 and 1991). Korchnoi is also a four-time USSR chess champion (1960, 1962, 1964–65, 1970), a five-time European champion, and a six-time member of Soviet teams that won the Chess Olympiad. In September 2006, he won the World Senior Chess Championship.

Oleg Alekseyevich **Protopopov** (b. June 16, 1932, in Leningrad (now St. Petersburg), Russia is a Russian-born figure skater. With his partner Ludmila **Belousova**, Protopopov won two gold medals in pairs at the Olympic Winter Games in 1964, in Innsbruck, Austria, and 1968, in Grenoble, and four World Championships in 1965, 1966, 1967 and 1968. In September 24, 1979, while Protopopov was touring in Europe, he defected with his partner Ludmila Belousova to Switzerland where they applied for political asylum. He currently lives in Switzerland.

Alexei Konstantinovich **Yagudin** born 18 March 1980) is a Russian figure skater. Born in Leningrad (now Saint Petersburg), Yagudin is the 2002 Olympic champion as well as a four-time World Champion, a two-time World Professional Figure Skating Champion, a three-time European Champion, and three- time Grand Prix Final gold medalist.

Evgeni Viktorovich Plushenko born November 3, 1982 in Solnechny, Khabarovsk Krai, Soviet Union (Russia) is a Russian figure skater, the seven-time National Champion, five-time European Champion, three- time World Champion, 2006 Winter Olympics gold medalist, and four-time Grand Prix Final gold medalist.

10. Epilogue

"I will be very sad if I ever happen to read a sign- board of an entertaining tavern or a French hotel for travelers on these Palazzos..." (Fyodor Dostoevsky)

CPSIA information can be obtained
at www.ICGtesting.com
Printed in the USA
LVHW072233200423
744869LV00002B/8

9781543773699